By Jane's Hand

Created by Emma O'Brien
with Olivia O'Brien

Crafted from the letters of Jane Austen,
Pride and Prejudice and songs of her time

CURRENCY PRESS
The performing arts publisher

LA MAMA

CURRENT THEATRE SERIES

First published in 2024
by Currency Press Pty Ltd,
Gadigal Land, Suite 310, 46–56 Kippax Street, Surry Hills, NSW 2010, Australia
enquiries@currency.com.au
www.currency.com.au

in association with La Mama

Typeset by Brighton Gray for Currency Press.
Cover image shows Olivia O'Brien; photo by Darren Gill; cover design by Mathias Johansson for Currency Press.

Currency Press acknowledges the Traditional Owners of the Country on which we live and work. We pay our respects to all Aboriginal and Torres Strait Islander Elders, past and present.

A catalogue record for this book is available from the National Library of Australia

Contents

Isha Menon, Marjorie Hannah and Olivia O'Brien in Seldom Theatre's production of By Jane's Hand *at La Mama, 2023 (Photo: Darren Gill)*

Olivia O'Brien and Isha Menon in Seldom Theatre's production of By Jane's Hand *at La Mama, 2023 (Photo: Darren Gill)*

By Jane's Hand was first produced by Seldom Theatre at La Mama Courthouse Theatre on the lands of the Kulin Nation, Melbourne, on 27 April 2023, with the following cast:

JANE ONE	Olivia O'Brien
JANE TWO	Isha Menon
JANE THREE	Marjorie Hannah

Director, Emma O'Brien
Set Designers, Emma O'Brien and Henry O'Brien
Lighting Designer, Hannah Willoughby
Sound Designer, Emma O'Brien
Costume Designer, Susan Halls
Set Builders, Martin Mason and Rod Connolly
Dramaturgs, Draf and Henry O'Brien

Olivia O'Brien, Marjorie Hannah and Isha Menon in Seldom Theatre's production of By Jane's Hand *at La Mama, 2023 (Photo: Darren Gill)*

Marjorie Hannah, Isha Menon and Olivia O'Brien in Seldom Theatre's production of By Jane's Hand *at La Mama, 2023 (Photo: Darren Gill)*

CHARACTERS

JANE ONE

JANE TWO

JANE THREE

The JANES also play characters from *Pride and Prejudice* within the world of the play. These are named in the script as 'JANE ONE AS MR DARCY', 'JANE ONE AS LIZZY', and so on. When text is named as 'ALL AS JANE', lines can be delivered in unison or by an individual JANE. **Bold text** is used in the script to indicate unison or echoes when two or more performers are playing a character simultaneously.

NOTE

By Jane's Hand is in three acts. The text is by Jane Austen drawn from her letters to her sister Cassandra and her timeless novel *Pride and Prejudice*. The spoken word is interspersed and underpinned with music that Jane Austen transcribed including folk songs, classical pieces, and bawdy alehouse tunes, all played live. The music reflects on, and guides, the narrative.

ACT ONE: 'DEAR CASSANDRA'—drawing on the texts from Jane's letters we establish a surreal Regency dreamscape to evoke being inside the magnificent mind of Jane Austen.

ACT TWO: 'DEAR ELIZABETH'—The characters of *Pride and Prejudice* come to life as the three JANES take turns evoking and playing the roles of LIZZY, MR DARCY, MR COLLINS, MR and MRS BENNET and LADY CATHERINE.

ACT THREE: 'DEAR JANE'—We return to Jane's letters and to her ailing health.

Isha Menon and Olivia O'Brien in Seldom Theatre's production of By Jane's Hand *at La Mama, 2023 (Photo: Darren Gill)*

SETTING

The style of the play is 'Surreal Regency' inside the magnificent mind of Jane Austen. The set is covered with material printed with stylised handwriting of excerpts of Austen's letters to Cassandra. There is a piano in a box, two stools, one chair, a dresser, and books around the edge of the performance space in various arrangements. The floor is painted like parchment paper. There are pieces of paper, in the same print, scrunched up across the floor. All three JANES wear Regency-style gowns made from material printed with the same text.

MUSIC

The music for the original production was scored for piano, harp, violin, Appalachian dulcimer, shruti box, penny whistle and three voices. Songs are presented in lyrics only in the text with basic melodic transcriptions and chordal structures provided as a resource; listed here in order of play: 'Catch: Joan Said to John' (Luffman Atterbury), 'It was a Pleasant Evening' (after the *Fairy Dance* by Holst), 'She Never Told Her Love' (Josef Haydn), 'Irishman' (William Shield, text by Robert Merry), 'Hot Cross Buns' (trad children's), 'Faint and Wearily' (Samuel James Arnold), 'Goosey Goosey Gander' (trad children's), 'Begone Dull Care' (anon), 'I Ha'e Laid a Herring in Salt' (trad anon), 'O Waly Waly' (trad anon), 'Let Us All Be Unhappy Together' (Charles Dibdin), 'Crazy Jane' (Harriet Abrams, text by Mr Lewis), 'Che Faro' (Christoph Willibald Gluck).

This play text went to press before the end of rehearsals and may differ from the play as performed.

Marjorie Hannah and Olivia O'Brien in Seldom Theatre's production of By Jane's Hand *at La Mama, 2023 (Photo: Darren Gill)*

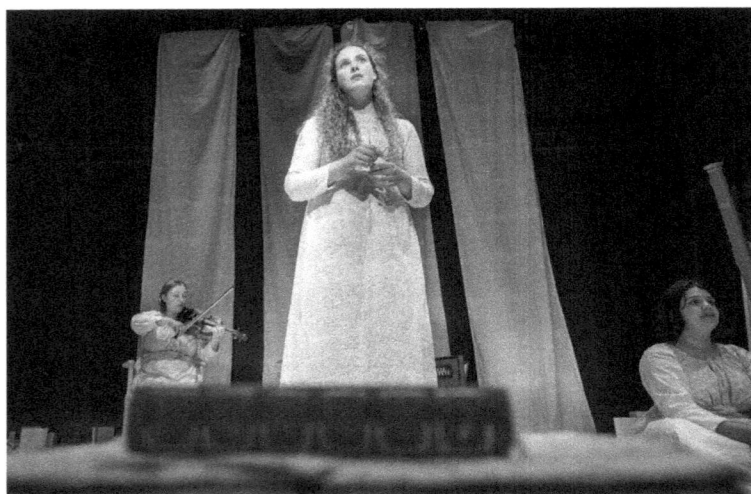

Marjorie Hannah, Olivia O'Brien and Isha Menon in Seldom Theatre's production of By Jane's Hand *at La Mama, 2023 (Photo: Darren Gill)*

ACT ONE: 'DEAR CASSANDRA'

SCENE ONE: THE OVERTURE

As the audience enters all JANES *are on stage. Mix of stage and house lights.*

JANE ONE *is at the piano practising her scales.* JANE TWO *is grabbing letters that are scrunched up and occasionally throwing them at the other* JANES. JANE THREE *is reading.*

Once the audience is fully seated the houselights are cued off when JANE TWO *throws a piece of paper at* JANE ONE. JANE ONE *begins to sing the 'Catch' below a capella and* JANE TWO *and* JANE THREE *join in on line two. The 'Catch' is sung as they move around the stage with energy.*

ALL AS JANE: [*sung*]
    Joan said to John, when he stop'd her t'other day,
    Pray John let me go, you know I cannot stay,
    Pray let me go, pray let me go, pray let me go, I cannot stay.
    You always so tease me and want me to stay,
    But tease me no more for now I must away,
    Tease me no more, tease me no more, tease me no more I must
        away.
    So, she left him in spite, of all, of all he could say,
    Who then could say nought, but nay Joan prithee stay,
    Nay prithee stay, Nay prithee stay, prithee stay, nay Joan prithee
        stay.

    *'*ALL AS JANE*' turn to the audience.*

JANE ONE: [*spoken like an upbeat*] Dear …

ALL AS JANE: Cassandra, I am very grand;

JANE TWO: indeed, I had the dignity of dropping out my mother's laudanum last night.

JANE ONE: I carry about the keys of the wine and closet,

JANE THREE: and twice since I began this letter have had orders to give in the kitchen.

ALL AS JANE: Our dinner was very good yesterday,

JANE THREE: and the chicken boiled perfectly tender; therefore,

JANE ONE: I shall not be obliged to dismiss Nanny on that account. Your loving sister

ALL AS JANE: Jane.

> *Beat.*

> *All* JANES *move to their instruments and begin to play small excerpts from the next piece of music as they speak.*

JANE ONE: Yes, yes, we have a pianoforte … as good as one that can be got for thirty Guineas …

JANE TWO: I returned from Manydown this morning; and found my mother certainly in no respect worse than when I left her. She does not like the cold weather, but that

ALL AS JANE: we cannot help.

JANE THREE: I had spent my time very quietly and very pleasantly with Catherine. Miss Blackford is agreeable enough.

JANE ONE: I do not want people to be very agreeable, as it saves me the trouble of liking them a great deal. Affectionately yours

ALL AS JANE: Jane.

SCENE TWO: MEET JANE

Next text section is scored for violin, piano and harp underpinning the dialogue.

JANE ONE: It was a pleasant evening.

JANE TWO: There were very few beauties, and such as there were; were not very handsome.

JANE THREE: Miss Iremonger did not look well, and Mrs Blount was the only one much admired.

JANE ONE: She appeared exactly as she did in September, with the same broad face,

JANE TWO: diamond bandeau,

JANE THREE: white shoes,

JANE TWO: [*sung*] pink husband, and

ALL AS JANE: fat neck.

JANE TWO *and* JANE THREE: The two Miss Coxes were there.

JANE TWO: I traced in one the remains of the vulgar, broad-featured girl who danced at Enham eight years ago;

JANE THREE: the other is refined into a nice, composed looking girl, like Catherine Bigg.

JANE ONE: Mrs Warren I was constrained to think a very fine young woman, which I much regret.

ALL AS JANE: [*as* JANE TWO *and* JANE THREE *dance a jig*] She danced away with great activity.

JANE ONE: Her husband is ugly enough

JANE TWO: uglier even than his cousin John;

JANE THREE: but he does not look so very old.

JANE ONE: Yours, Jane.

> *Beat.*

Dear Cassandra, tell Mary that I make over Mr Heartley and all his estate to her for her sole use and benefit in future,

JANE ONE: [*sung with violin and harp accompaniment*]
> She never told her love,
> She never told her love,
> But let concealment, like a worm in the bud,
> Feed on her damask cheek.

JANE TWO: [*spoken whilst playing an accompanying instrument*] and she can have not only him, but all my other admirers into the bargain wherever she can find them,

JANE ONE: [*sung*]
> She sat, like Patience on a monument,
> Smiling, smiling at grief,
> Smiling, smiling at grief,

JANE TWO: [*spoken*] even the kiss which C. Powlett wanted to give me,

JANE THREE: as I mean to confine myself in future to Mr Tom Lefroy,

ALL AS JANE: for whom I do not care sixpence.

> *Beat.*

JANE ONE: Assure her also, as a last and indubitable proof of Warren's indifference to me, that

JANE THREE: he actually drew that gentleman's picture for

JANE TWO: me

JANE ONE: me,

JANE THREE: me
JANE ONE: and delivered it
JANE THREE: to me
JANE ONE: me
JANE TWO: me
JANE ONE: without a sigh.

> *Beat.*

> [*Sung.*]
> The London folks themselves beguile

JANE TWO: [*sung*]

> and think they please in a capital style.

JANE TWO: [*sung*]

> Yet let them ask as they cross the street,

JANE ONE: [*sung*]

> of any young virgin they happen to meet.

JANE THREE: [*sung*]

> And I know she'll say from behind her Fan,

JANE ONE: [*sung*]

> that there's none can love like an Irishman.

ALL AS JANE: [*sung*]

> There's none can love, love, love: like an Irishman, like an Irishman,
> There's none can love like an Irishman.

> *Beat.*

> [*Spoken*] Dear Cassandra,

JANE THREE: You scold me so much in the nice long letter which I have this moment received from you,
JANE ONE: that I am almost afraid to tell you how my Irish friend and I behaved.
JANE TWO: Imagine to yourself everything most profligate,
ALL AS JANE: and shocking
JANE ONE: in the way of dancing
JANE THREE: and sitting down together.
ALL AS JANE [*sung*]

> Like an Irishman, like an Irishman, here's none can love like an Irishman.

> *Beat.*

JANE TWO: [*spoken direct to an audience member*] Martha sends her love and hopes to have the pleasure of seeing you when you return.

JANE ONE: You are to understand this message as being merely for the sake of a message to oblige me.

JANE THREE: I rather expect to receive an offer from my friend in the course of the evening.

JANE ONE: I shall refuse him, however,

JANE TWO: unless he promises to give away his White Coat,

ALL AS JANE: [*sung a capella*]

> One a penny, two a penny, Hot cross buns
> One a penny, two a penny, Hot cross buns
> If you have no daughters, if you have no daughters,
> If you have no daughters, pray give them to your sons
> But if you have none of these little elves, these little elves
> Then you may eat them, then you may eat them
> Eat them, eat them, eat them, eat them
> Then you may eat them all yourselves

Beat.

This next section is acted out like a small play within the play with gestures in the tradition of the Austen family (until the close of the song).

[*Spoken*] Dear Cassandra,

JANE TWO: I should have begun my letter soon after our arrival, but for a little adventure which prevented me.

JANE THREE: After we had been here a quarter of an hour it was discovered that my writing and dressing boxes had been by accident put into a chaise,

JANE ONE: which was just packing off as we came in,

JANE THREE: and were driven away toward Gravesend in their way to the West Indies.

JANE ONE: No part of my property could have been such a prize before, for in my writing box was all my worldly wealth.

ALL AS JANE: [*sung with accompaniment*]

> Faint and wearily the wayworn traveller,
> Plods uncheerily afraid to stop.

JANE THREE: [*spoken*] Mr Nottley immediately despatched a man and horse after the chaise,

ALL AS JANE: [*sung*]

> Wand'ring drearily, a sad unraveller,
> Of the mazes toward the mountain top.
> Doubting fear while his course he's steering,
> Cottages appearing as he's nigh to drop.

JANE ONE: [*spoken*] and in half an hour's time I had the pleasure of being as rich as ever; they were got about two or three miles off.

ALL AS JANE [*sung*]

> Oh! how briskly then, the wayworn traveller
> Treads the mazes toward the mountain top.

> *Beat.*

JANE TWO: [*spoken*] Cassandra, you express so little anxiety about my being murdered under Ash Park Copse by Mr Hulbert's servant that I have a great mind not to tell whether I was or not,

JANE ONE: and shall only say that I did not return home that night or the next,

JANE THREE: as Martha kindly made room for me in her bed.

JANE ONE: The bed did exceedingly well for us,

JANE TWO: both to lie awake in and talk till two o'clock,

JANE THREE: and to sleep in the rest of the night,

JANE ONE: I love Martha, better than ever.

ALL AS JANE: [*sung a capella*]

> Dear sweet somebody

> *Beat.*

> JANE TWO *and* JANE THREE *start to conduct an imaginary orchestra,* JANE ONE *moves to the piano.*

JANE TWO: [*spoken*] There is to be a grand gala on Tuesday evening in Sydney Gardens,

JANE THREE: a concert,

JANE ONE: with illuminations

ALL AS JANE: and fireworks.

JANE ONE: To the latter, Elizabeth and I look forward with pleasure, and even the concert will have more than its usual charm for me, as the gardens are large enough for me to get pretty well beyond the reach of its sound.

JANE THREE: In the morning Lady Willoughby is to present the colours to some corps, or Yeomanry, or other, in the Crescent, and that such festivities may have a proper commencement.

> JANE ONE *on the piano plays a pompous 'da da da daaa' and* JANE TWO *and* JANE THREE *play mock trumpets which then transform into a children's hand-clapping game under the next six lines of dialogue.*

JANE TWO: I have received my aunt's letter; and thank you for your scrap.

JANE THREE: for your scrap

JANE TWO: I will write to Charles soon. Pray give Fanny and Edward

JANE THREE: a kiss from me

JANE TWO: and ask George if he has got a new

JANE TWO *and* JANE THREE: song for me.

> *Beat.*

> *Clapping game transforms,* JANE TWO *and* JANE THREE *begin to dance and a start a dramatic 'dip'.*

JANE ONE: At length, the day is come on which I am to flirt my last with Tom Lefroy, and

ALL AS JANE: when you receive this,

JANE ONE: it will be over.

JANE TWO: [*mockingly swoons and* JANE THREE *catches them*] My tears flow as I write at the melancholy idea.

> *Beat.*

> JANE THREE *suddenly drops* JANE TWO *on the floor.*

> JANE THREE *unceremoniously steps over them.*

JANE THREE: I am quite pleased with Martha and Mrs Lefroy for wanting the pattern of our caps, but I am not so well pleased with your giving it to them.

> JANE ONE *helps* JANE TWO *off the ground.*

JANE ONE: Some wish, some prevailing wish, is necessary to the animation of everybody's mind,

JANE THREE: and in gratifying this you leave them to form some other wish

JANE TWO looks angrily at JANE THREE *as they rub their lower back from the fall/drop*

JANE TWO: which will not probably be half so innocent.

Beat.

All the JANES *begin to pick up and examine different letters/ writings that are scrunched up on the ground. They may read them as items of news or as manuscript. All the* JANES *remove them from the playing area of the stage throughout this spoken text and song. By the end of this act there are no more pieces of scrunched paper on stage.*

JANE ONE: Cassandra, Chute called here yesterday. I wonder what he means by being so civil.

JANE THREE: There is a report that Tom is going to be married to a Lichfield lass.

JANE ONE: [*sings/hums half underneath*]
and I know she'll say behind her fan, there's none can love like a

Stops suddenly.

Cassandra, I would not let Martha read my manuscript of *First Impressions* again upon any account and am very glad that I did not leave it in your power.

ALL AS JANE: She is very cunning,

JANE ONE: but I saw through her design;

JANE THREE: she means to publish it from memory,

JANE TWO: and one more perusal must enable her to do it.

ALL AS JANE: [*sung in three-part harmony*]
Joan said to John, when he stop'd her t'other day,
Pray John let me go, you know I cannot stay,
Pray let me go, pray let me go, pray let me go, I cannot stay.
You always so tease me and want me to stay,
But tease me no more for now I must away,
Tease me no more, tease me no more, tease me no more I must away.
So, she left him in spite, of all, of all he could say,
Who then could say nought, but nay Joan prithee stay,
Nay prithee stay, Nay prithee stay, prithee stay, nay Joan prithee stay.

ACT TWO: 'DEAR ELIZABETH'

Objects are used throughout this act for character transformation. In the original production the following was used: a hat for MR DARCY, *a book for* LIZZY, *a long piece of material like a piece of adornment worn by clergy for* MR COLLINS, *a wig for* LADY CATHERINE.

SCENE ONE: THEY COME TO LIFE

JANE ONE: [*spoken*] It is a truth ... it is a truth acknowledged ... it is a truth universally acknowledged ... that a man ...

There are few people whom I really love, and still fewer of whom I think well.

JANE TWO: The more I see of the world,

JANE THREE: the more am I dissatisfied

ALL AS JANE: with it;

JANE ONE: and every day confirms my belief of the inconsistency of all human characters, and of

ALL AS JANE: the little dependence

JANE ONE: that can be placed

JANE TWO: on the appearance

JANE THREE: of merit

JANE ONE: or sense.

Beat.

In this section, three roles are constant: JANE ONE *is* JANE, JANE TWO *is* MR DARCY, JANE THREE *is* LIZZY.

JANE *speaks as if to conjure* MR DARCY.

From the very beginning—from the first moment, I may almost say—of my acquaintance with you, your manners, impressing me with the fullest belief of your arrogance, your conceit, and your selfish distain of the feelings of others, were such as to form the groundwork of the disapprobation on which succeeding events have built so immovable a dislike.

JANE TWO AS MR DARCY *looks confused.* JANE ONE *encourages them to speak in response almost conducting them.*

JANE TWO AS MR DARCY: [*without conviction*] My good opinion once lost, is lost forever.

JANE ONE: [*getting annoyed*] your selfish disdain of the feelings of others …

JANE TWO AS MR DARCY: [*over the top this time*] My good opinion once lost, is lost forever!

JANE THREE AS LIZZY: [*whilst sitting and reading the book*] Vanity and pride are different things,

JANE ONE: though the words are often used synonymously.

JANE THREE AS LIZZY: A person may be proud without being vain.

JANE ONE: [*to* MR DARCY *whilst placing the hat on their head*] Pride relates more to our opinion of ourselves, vanity to what we would have others think of us.

JANE TWO AS MR DARCY: [*cool and smouldering*] My good opinion once lost, is lost forever. [*Continuing and starting to address this to* JANE] In vain have I struggled. It will not do. My feelings will not be repressed. You must allow me to tell you how ardently I admire and love you.

JANE THREE AS LIZZY *is reading and ignoring* MR DARCY.

JANE ONE: Elizabeth—

She moves to JANE THREE *prompting them to stand and become engaged in the dialogue with* MR DARCY.

—had a lively, playful disposition, which delighted in anything ridiculous.

JANE TWO AS MR DARCY: [*to both*] She is tolerable, but not handsome enough to tempt me

JANE ONE: [*to* JANE THREE AS LIZZY] I am perfectly convinced by it that Mr Darcy has no defect. He owns it himself without disguise.

JANE TWO AS MR DARCY: [*to* JANE] No, I have made no such pretension. I have faults enough, but they are not, I hope, of understanding. I cannot forget the follies and vices of others so soon as I ought, nor their offenses against myself. My feelings are not puffed about with every attempt to move them. My temper would perhaps be called resentful.

JANE ONE: [*completing his line so they cut across him*] Yes and your good opinion once lost, is lost forever.

JANE THREE AS LIZZY: That is a failing indeed! Implacable resentment is a shade in a character. But you have chosen your fault well. I really cannot laugh at it. You are safe from me.

JANE TWO AS MR DARCY: There is, I believe, in every disposition a tendency to some evil—a natural defect, which not even the best education can overcome.

JANE THREE AS LIZZY: [*without venom*] And your defect is to hate everybody.

JANE TWO AS MR DARCY: [*smiling to* JANE *and* JANE *as* LIZZY] And yours, is wilfully to misunderstand them.

> JANE ONE *starts to sing and play on the dulcimer to encourage* MR DARCY *and* LIZZY *to connect, one by one they break character and come and sing with* JANE ONE.

JANE ONE: [*sung with dulcimer*]
Were I obliged to beg my bread?
And had not where to lay my head.
I'd creep where yonder flocks are fed,
And steal a look at Somebody, Poor, dear Somebody,
Dear, sweet Somebody.
Oh, had I eagles wings to fly,
I'd bend my course across the sky.
And soon bestow one loving eye,
On my adored somebody, poor dear somebody.
Dear sweet somebody

ALL AS JANE: [*sung*]
Oh, had I eagles wings to fly,
I'd bend my course across the sky.
And soon bestow one loving eye,
On my adored somebody, poor dear somebody
Dear sweet somebody.

> *Beat.*

> *In this section* JANE ONE *is* JANE, LIZZY *and* MR COLLINS, JANE TWO *is* LIZZY *and* MR COLLINS, *and* JANE THREE *is* LIZZY *and* MR COLLINS.

JANE ONE: [*contemplating the character who will be revealed as* JANE THREE AS MR COLLINS, *spoken*] Odious man, nothing can clear Mr Collins from the guilt of inheriting Longbourn, he may turn you all out of this house as soon as he pleases.

JANE THREE AS MR COLLINS: [*wearing the object for* MR COLLINS *and speaking obsequiously*] I have frequently wished to heal the breach.

JANE ONE: [*to* JANE TWO AS LIZZY, *and holding the book*] Oddity. I cannot make him out.

JANE THREE AS MR COLLINS: I have been so fortunate as to be distinguished by the patronage of the Right Honourable Lady Catherine de Bourgh, whose bounty and beneficence has preferred me to the valuable rectory of this parish.

JANE TWO AS LIZZY: [*to* JANE ONE AS JANE] There is something very pompous in his style. Absurd, not a sensible man, and the deficiency of nature had been, but little assisted by education or society.

JANE THREE AS MR COLLINS: I am very sensible, madam, of the hardship to my fair cousins, and could say much on the subject, but that I am cautious of appearing forward and precipitate.

JANE ONE: [*sizing up* JANE THREE AS MR COLLINS] But he was now a good deal counteracted by the self-conceit of a weak head,

JANE TWO AS LIZZY: a mixture of pride

JANE ONE: and obsequiousness,

JANE TWO AS LIZZY: self-importance,

JANE ONE: and humility.

JANE THREE AS MR COLLINS: [*moving towards* JANE ONE *and* JANE TWO AS LIZZY] But I can assure the young ladies that I come prepared to admire them. At present I will not say more; but, perhaps, when we are better acquainted.

JANE ONE AS MR COLLINS: [*taking the object over from* JANE THREE] I have more than once observed to Lady Catherine that her charming daughter seemed born to be a duchess, and that the most elevated rank, instead of giving her consequence, would be adorned by her. These are the kind of little things which please her ladyship, and it is a sort of attention which I conceive myself peculiarly bound to pay.

JANE TWO AS LIZZY: It is happy for you that you possess the talent of flattering with delicacy.

JANE THREE AS LIZZY: [*now has the book*] May I ask whether these pleasing attentions proceed from the impulse of the moment, or are the result of previous study?

JANE ONE AS MR COLLINS : They arise chiefly from what is passing at the time, and though I sometimes amuse myself with suggesting and arranging such little elegant compliments as may be adapted to ordinary occasions, I always wish to give them as unstudied an air as possible.

JANE ONE AS MR COLLINS: [*amorously*] Ahh Jane …

JANE ONE AS MR COLLINS: Ahhhh Elizabeth!

> JANE ONE *and* JANE TWO *play* MR COLLINS *simultaneously. The one who isn't leading speaks the* **bold text** *in unison or as an echo.*
>
> *Both* JANE ONE *and* JANE TWO *have the* MR COLLINS *object and are moving towards* JANE THREE.

Elizabeth … Believe me, my **dear Miss Elizabeth**,

JANE TWO AS MR COLLINS: that your modesty, so far from doing you any disservice, rather adds to your other **perfections.** You would have been less amiable in my eyes had there not been this **little unwillingness**; but allow me to **assure you**, that I have your respected **mother's permission** for this address. You can hardly doubt the purport of my discourse. Almost as soon as **I entered** the house, I singled you out as the **companion** of my future life.

JANE ONE AS MR COLLINS: But before I am run away with by my **feelings** on this subject, perhaps it would be advisable for me to state my reasons for **marrying** and, moreover, for **coming** into Hertfordshire with the design of **selecting a wife**, as I certainly did. My reasons for **marrying** are, first,

JANE TWO AS MR COLLINS: that I think it a right thing for every clergyman in easy circumstances, like myself,

JANE ONE AS MR COLLINS: myself,

JANE TWO AS MR COLLINS: to set the example of **matrimony** in his **parish**; secondly,

JANE ONE AS MR COLLINS: that I am convinced that it will add very greatly to my **happiness** and thirdly,

JANE TWO AS MR COLLINS: which perhaps I ought to have mentioned earlier, but the fact is, that being, as I am, to **inherit** this estate after the **death** of your honoured father, I could not **satisfy myself** without resolving to choose a **wife** from among his **daughters.**

JANE ONE AS MR COLLINS: This has been my motive, my **fair cousin,** and I flatter myself it will not **sink** me in your esteem.

JANE TWO AS MR COLLINS: And now nothing **remains** for me but to **assure** you in the most animated language of the **violence** of my **affection**.

JANE ONE *and* JANE THREE AS LIZZY: It is absolutely necessary to interrupt him now!

JANE THREE AS LIZZY: [*emphatically*] You are too hasty, sir. You forget that I have made no answer. Let me do it without further loss of time. Accept my thanks for the compliment you are paying me. I am very sensible of the honour of your proposals, but it is impossible for me to do otherwise than to decline them.

JANE TWO AS MR COLLINS: I am not now to learn, that it is usual with young ladies to reject the addresses of the man whom they secretly mean to accept, when he first applies for their favour; and that sometimes the refusal is repeated a second, or even a third time. I am therefore by no means discouraged by what you have just said and shall hope to lead you to the altar ere long.

JANE ONE AS LIZZY: Upon my word, sir

They take the book from JANE THREE.

I am perfectly serious in my refusal. You could not make me happy, and I am convinced that I am the last woman in the world who could make you so.

JANE THREE AS MR COLLINS *joins* JANE TWO AS MR COLLINS *with the object now around* JANE TWO *and* JANE THREE.

JANE THREE AS MR COLLINS: I shall hope to receive a more favourable answer than you have now given me; though I am far from accusing you of **cruelty** at present, because I know it to be the established **custom** of your **sex** to reject a man on the first **application,**

JANE TWO AS MR COLLINS: and perhaps you have even now said as much to encourage my **suit**

They place the MR COLLINS *object around* JANE ONE AS LIZZY.

All JANES *are now* MR COLLINS *and follow the convention of the unison or echoes with the bolded text.*

JANE ONE AS MR COLLINS: [*as they transform to* MR COLLINS] as would be consistent with the true delicacy of the **female character**. You must give me leave to **flatter myself**, my dear cousin, that your refusal of my addresses is merely words of course, and you should take it into further consideration, that in spite of your **manifold attractions**,

JANE TWO AS MR COLLINS: it is by no means certain that another offer of **marriage** may ever be made to you.

JANE ONE AS MR COLLINS: I must therefore conclude that you are **not serious** in your **rejection** of me, I shall choose to attribute it to your wish of **increasing** my love by **suspense**, according to the usual practice of **elegant females.**

ALL AS MR COLLINS: [*sung a capella*]
> Goosey Goosey Gander, whither shall I wander?
> Upstairs and downstairs, in my Lady's chamber.
> Old father long legs would not say his prayers, old father long legs would not say his prayers

ALL AS JANE: [*sung*]
> Take him by the left leg, take him by the left leg, take him by the left leg and throw him down stairs.

> JANE TWO *uses puppets to represent* MR BENNET *and* MRS BENNET.

JANE TWO AS MRS BENNET: [*spoken*] Mr Bennet, you are wanted immediately; we are all in an uproar. You must come and make Lizzy marry Mr Collins, for she vows she will not have him, and if you do not make haste, he will change his mind and not have her.

JANE TWO AS MR BENNET: Come here, child, I have sent for you on an affair of importance. An unhappy alternative is before you, Elizabeth. From this day you must be a stranger to one of your parents. Your mother will never see you again if you do not marry Mr Collins, and I will never see you again if you do.

ALL AS LIZZY: [*sung with piano*]
> Begone, dull care, I prithee be gone from me.
> Begone, dull care, you and I shall never agree.
> Long-time thou hast been vexing me and fain thou would'st me kill.

But in faith, dull care
Thou never shall have thy will.

Beat.

JANE ONE AS MR DARCY *takes up their position waiting to dance with* JANE THREE AS LIZZY, *both have their character's objects.*

SCENE TWO: WEAVING IN AND OUT

JANE ONE *is* MR DARCY *and* LIZZY, JANE TWO *is* JANE *and* LIZZY, JANE THREE *is* LIZZY *and* MR DARCY. *All objects are passed between the* JANES *as they swap characters.*

JANE ONE AS MR DARCY: [*spoken*] May I have the next dance, Miss Elizabeth?

JANE THREE AS LIZZY: [*moving towards* MR DARCY] You may.

JANE TWO: They stood for some time without speaking a word; and she began to imagine that their silence was to last through the two dances, and at first was resolved not to break it; till suddenly fancying that it would be the greater punishment to her partner to oblige him to talk. After a pause of some minutes …

JANE TWO *opens a music box with a dance tune and encourages them to dance and begins to compete for the role of* LIZZY *with* JANE THREE *which includes snatching the book from one another.*

JANE THREE AS LIZZY: It is your turn to say something now, Mr Darcy. I talked about the dance, and you ought to make some sort of remark on the size of the room, or the number of couples.

JANE TWO AS LIZZY: Perhaps by and by

JANE THREE AS LIZZY: I may observe that private balls are much pleasanter than public ones.

JANE ONE AS MR DARCY: Do you talk by rule, then, while you are dancing?

JANE TWO AS LIZZY: Sometimes.

JANE THREE AS LIZZY: We are each of an unsocial, taciturn disposition,

JANE TWO AS LIZZY: unwilling to speak, unless we expect to say

JANE TWO AS LIZZY: something that will amaze the whole room,

JANE THREE AS LIZZY: and be handed down to posterity with all the éclat of a proverb.

JANE ONE AS MR DARCY *is confused.*

JANE TWO: [*leading* JANE ONE AS MR DARCY *to engage*] Do you and your …

JANE ONE AS MR DARCY: your sisters often walk to Meryton?

JANE TWO: [*leading* JANE THREE LIZZY] Yes, when you met us there the other day …

JANE THREE AS LIZZY: … the other day we had just been forming a new acquaintance.

JANE ONE AS MR DARCY: [*turns away and slams the music box shut*] Wickham! Mr Wickham is blessed with such happy manners as may ensure his making friends. Whether he may be equally capable of retaining them, is less certain.

JANE TWO AS LIZZY: He has been so unlucky as to lose your friendship.

JANE THREE AS LIZZY: And in a manner which he is likely to suffer from all his life.

JANE ONE AS LIZZY: I remember hearing you once say, Mr Darcy, that you hardly ever forgave, that your resentment once created was unappeasable.

JANE TWO: And you never allow yourself to be blinded by prejudice?

JANE THREE AS MR DARCY: I hope not. May I ask to what these questions tend?

JANE ONE AS LIZZY: Merely to the illustration of your character

JANE TWO: I am trying to make it out.

JANE ONE AS LIZZY: I hear such different accounts of you

JANE TWO: as puzzle me exceedingly [*she gestures to* JANE]

JANE TWO: [*sung with dulcimer*]
   I Ha'e laid a herring in salt …

JANE THREE AS MR DARCY: [*sung*]
   Lass gin ye lo'e me, tell me now …

JANE TWO: [*sung*]
   I ha'e brew'd a forpit of malt …

JANE ONE AS LIZZY: [*sung*]
   And I canna come-ilka day to woo …

JANE THREE AS MR DARCY: [*sung*]
   I ha'e a calf will soon be a cow,

JANE TWO: [*sung*]
   Lass gin ye lo'e me, tell me now.

JANE ONE AS LIZZY: [*sung*]
> I ha'e pig will soon be a sow,

ALL AS JANE: [*sung*]
> And I canna come-ilka day to woo.

ALL AS JANE: [*sung as they all dance together*]
> I've ha'e a hen with happity leg,
> Lass gin ye lo'e me, tak' me now.
> Which ilka day lays me an egg,
> And I canna come-ilka day to woo.
> I ha'e a cabbage upon my shelf,
> Lass gin ye lo'e me, tak' me now.
> I downa eat it a 'myself,
> And I canna come-ilka day to woo.

> *Beat.*

> JANE ONE *is* JANE *and* LIZZY, JANE TWO *is* MR DARCY, JANE THREE *is* JANE *and* LIZZY.

JANE THREE: [*spoken*] In a hurried manner he immediately began an enquiry after her health.

JANE ONE: He sat down for a few moments,

> JANE TWO AS MR DARCY *sits on the book for* LIZZY *and takes it with them.*

JANE TWO AS MR DARCY: and then getting up, walked about the room.

JANE THREE: After a silence of several minutes,

JANE TWO AS MR DARCY: he came towards her in an agitated manner, and thus began. In vain I have struggled. It will not do. My feelings will not be repressed. You must allow me to tell you how ardently I admire and love you.

JANE ONE *and* JANE THREE: He spoke well.

JANE ONE: But there were feelings besides those of the heart to be detailed; and he was not more eloquent on the subject of tenderness than of pride.

JANE THREE: His sense of her inferiority, of its being a degradation, of the family obstacles which had always opposed him to inclination.

JANE ONE: He concluded with representing to her the strength of that attachment which, in spite of all his endeavours, he had found

JANE TWO AS MR DARCY: impossible to conquer;

JANE ONE: and with expressing his hope that it would now be rewarded by her acceptance of his hand.

Short beat.

JANE THREE AS LIZZY: [*to* JANE TWO AS MR DARCY] I would now thank you. But I cannot. I have never desired your good opinion, and you have certainly bestowed it most unwillingly.

JANE ONE AS LIZZY: [*to* JANE TWO AS MR DARCY] I might as well enquire, why with so evident a desire of offending and insulting me, you chose to tell me that you liked me against your will, against your reason, and even against your character? I have every reason in the world to think ill of you.

JANE TWO AS MR DARCY: [*to both*] And this is your opinion of me! My faults, according to this calculation, are heavy indeed! But perhaps these offenses might have been overlooked, had not your pride been hurt by my honest confession of the scruples that had long prevented my forming any serious design.

JANE TWO AS MR DARCY *and* JANE THREE AS JANE: Could you expect me to rejoice in the inferiority of your connections?

JANE ONE AS LIZZY: You are mistaken, Mr Darcy, if you suppose that the mode of your declaration affected me in any other way, than as it spared me the concern which I might have felt in refusing you,

JANE THREE: had you behaved in a more gentlemanlike manner.

JANE ONE AS LIZZY: You could not have made the offer of your hand

JANE THREE: in any possible way

JANE ONE AS LIZZY: that would have tempted me to accept it.

JANE TWO AS MR DARCY *and* JANE ONE AS LIZZY: I had not known you a month

JANE ONE AS LIZZY: before I felt that you were the last man in the world whom I could ever be prevailed on to marry.

Beat.

SCENE THREE: A PASTORAL RELIEF

JANE ONE AS JANE, JANE THREE AS JANE *and* LIZZY, JANE TWO AS JANE *and* LADY CATHERINE.

A violin drone begins played by JANE THREE *under the stillness until* JANE ONE *breaks character from being* LIZZY. JANE TWO *remains* MR DARCY *until line three of the song and then breaks.*

JANE ONE: [*sung with violin, harmony can be sung by* JANE THREE]
O Waly, waly up yon bank
and waly waly down yon brae,
and waly by yon river side
where I and my love wont to gae.
O waly, waly, Love is bonny
a little while when it is new;
but when it auld it waxes cauld
and wears away like morning dew.

The melody for 'Waly Waly' continues underneath the next lines and breaks on LADY CATHERINE'*s untimely entry.*

JANE ONE: [*spoken*] Pemberley House, situated on the opposite side of a valley, was a large, handsome stone building, standing well on rising ground, Elizabeth was delighted.

JANE TWO AS LADY CATHERINE: [*interrupts music wearing the wig object*] Heaven and earth! Of what are you thinking? Are the shades of Pemberley to be thus polluted?

JANE ONE *and* JANE THREE *shoo her away.*

JANE TWO AS LADY CATHERINE: Upon my word [*Straight to* JANE ONE] you give your opinion very decidedly for so young a person.

JANE ONE *ignores* JANE TWO AS LADY CATHERINE *as a violin begins to play again under the spoken word.*

JANE ONE: Every disposition of the ground was good; and she looked on the whole scene, the river, the trees scattered on its banks and the winding of the valley, as far as she could trace it, with delight.

JANE THREE AS LIZZY: And of this place, I might have been mistress! With these rooms I might now have been familiarly acquainted!

JANE ONE: Instead of viewing them as a stranger,

JANE TWO: I might have rejoiced in them as my own, and welcomed to them as visitors, my uncle and aunt.

JANE ONE: But no, that could never be;

JANE TWO: my uncle and aunt would have been lost to me;

JANE THREE AS LIZZY: I should not have been allowed to invite them.

JANE ONE: That was a lucky recollection, it saved you from something very like regret.

Reprise 'Waly Waly' with violin and harp.

JANE ONE *and* JANE TWO: [*sung*]
    When cockleshells turn silver bells,
    And mussels grow on ev'ry tree;
    When frost and snaw shall warm us a',
    Then shall my Love prove true to me.
    But had I wist before I kiss'd
    That love had been sae ill to win;
    I'd lockt my heart in case of gold,
    And pin'd it with a silver pin.

Beat.

SCENE FOUR: A LADY CACOPHONY

For this section All JANES *play* LADY CATHERINE *and* JANE ONE *and* JANE THREE *are* LIZZY. *Bolded words can be in unison or echoed when more than one* JANE *is playing* LADY CATHERINE *at the same time (*JANE TWO *is always* LADY CATHERINE). *All wear the wigs when playing* LADY CATHERINE *(there are three identical wigs).*

JANE TWO AS LADY CATHERINE: [*spoken*] You can be at no loss, Miss Bennet, to understand the reason of my journey hither. Your own heart, your own conscience, must tell you why I come.

JANE THREE AS LIZZY: [*holding the book*] Indeed, you are mistaken, Madam. I have not been at all able to account for the honour of seeing you here.

JANE ONE AS LADY CATHERINE: Miss Bennet, you ought to know, that I am not to be trifled with. But however insincere you may choose to be, you shall not find me so. My character has ever been celebrated for its sincerity and frankness, and in a cause of such moment as this, I shall certainly not depart from it.

JANE ONE *and* JANE TWO AS LADY CATHERINE: **A report of a most alarming nature reached me two days ago,**

JANE THREE AS LADY CATHERINE: That **you,** that Miss Elizabeth Bennet, would, in all likelihood, be soon afterwards united to **my nephew, my own nephew**, Mr Darcy. Though I know it must be a **scandalous falsehood**, though I would not **injure him** so much as to suppose the truth **of it possible,** I instantly resolved on setting off for **this place**, that I might make my sentiments known **to you.**

JANE ONE AS LIZZY: If you believed it impossible to be true, I wonder you took the trouble of coming so far. What could your ladyship propose by it?

JANE TWO AS LADY CATHERINE: **At once to insist** upon having such a report universally **contradicted**.

JANE THREE AS LIZZY: Your coming to Longbourn, will be rather a confirmation of it; if, indeed, such a report is in existence.

JANE ONE AS LADY CATHERINE: Do you then pretend to be **ignorant of it**? And can you likewise declare that there is no foundation for it?

JANE ONE *and* JANE TWO AS LADY CATHERINE: **This is not to be borne, not to be borne, not to be borne!**

JANE THREE AS LADY CATHERINE: Miss Bennet, I insist on being satisfied. Has he, has my nephew, made you an offer of marriage?

JANE ONE AS LIZZY: Your ladyship has declared it to be impossible.

JANE THREE AS LADY CATHERINE: Miss Bennet, do you know who I am? I have not been accustomed to such language as this. I am almost the nearest **relation he has** in the world and am **entitled to know** all his dearest concerns.

JANE ONE AS LIZZY: But you are not entitled to know mine; nor will such behaviour as this, ever induce me to be explicit.

JANE TWO AS LADY CATHERINE: Let me be rightly understood. This match, to which you have the presumption to aspire, can never take place.

JANE THREE AS LADY CATHERINE: No, never. Mr Darcy is engaged to my daughter.

JANE TWO AS LADY CATHERINE: Now what have you to say?

JANE ONE AS LIZZY: Only this; that if he is so, you can have no reason to suppose he will make an offer to me.

JANE TWO *and* JANE THREE AS LADY CATHERINE: Obstinate, headstrong girl!

JANE THREE AS LADY CATHERINE: Tell me once for all, are you engaged to him?

JANE ONE AS LIZZY: I am not.

JANE TWO AS LADY CATHERINE: And will you promise me, never to enter into such an engagement?

JANE ONE AS LIZZY: I will make no promise of the kind.

JANE TWO AS LADY CATHERINE: Heaven and earth!—

JANE THREE AS LADY CATHERINE: Of what are you thinking?

ALL JANES AS LADY CATHERINE: **Are the shades of Pemberley to be thus polluted?**

> *Reprise 'Herring in Salt'.* JANE ONE *sings a capella, defiantly, with a rhythmic foot stomp.*

JANE ONE AS LIZZY: [*sung*]
> I Ha'e laid a herring in salt,
> Lass gin ye lo'e me, tell me now.
> I ha'e brew'd a forpit of malt,
> And I canna come—ilka day to woo.
> I ha'e a calf will soon be a cow,
> Lass gin ye lo'e me, tell me now.
> I ha'e pig will soon be a sow,
> And I canna come—ilka day to woo.

[*Spoken, exhilarated and exhausted*] You can now have nothing farther to say.

JANE TWO *and* JANE THREE AS LADY CATHERINE: **You are then resolved to have him?**

JANE ONE AS LIZZY: I have said no such thing.

JANE ONE AS JANE: I am only resolved to act in that manner, which will, in my own opinion, constitute my happiness, without reference to you, or to any person so wholly unconnected with me.

JANE TWO AS JANE: [*removes wig*] with me.

JANE THREE AS JANE: [*removes wig*] with me.

SCENE FIVE: A TIMELESS RECAPITULATION

JANE ONE *is* JANE, JANE TWO *is* MR DARCY *and* LIZZY, JANE THREE *is* MR DARCY *and* LIZZY.

ALL AS JANE: [*sung a capella*]
　　We're I obliged to beg my bread?
　　And had not where to lay my head,
　　I'd creep where yonder flocks are fed,
　　And steal a look at somebody, poor, dear somebody, dear, sweet
　　　　somebody.

JANE TWO AS MR DARCY: [*spoken to the audience*] You are too generous to trifle with me. If your feelings are still what they were last April, tell me so at once.

JANE THREE AS MR DARCY: [*to the audience*] My affections and wishes are unchanged; but one word from you will silence me on this subject for ever.

JANE ONE: [*to the audience*] Elizabeth, feeling all the more than common awkwardness and anxiety of his situation, now forced herself to speak; and immediately, though not very fluently, gave him to understand that her sentiments had undergone so material a change, since the period to which he alluded, as to make her receive with gratitude and pleasure his present assurances. The happiness which this reply produced, was such as he had probably never felt before; and he expressed himself on the occasion as sensibly and as warmly as a man violently in love can be supposed to do.

JANE TWO AS LIZZY: [*to* JANE ONE] Perhaps I did not always love him so well as I do now.

JANE THREE AS LIZZY: [*to* JANE ONE] But in such cases as these, a good memory is unpardonable.

JANE TWO AS LIZZY: [*to* JANE ONE] This is the last time I shall ever remember it myself.

JANE ONE: [*to* JANE TWO *and* JANE THREE] Or, in other words, you are determined to have him. He is rich, to be sure, and you may have more fine clothes and fine carriages than Jane. But will they make you happy?

JANE THREE AS LIZZY: Have you any other objection than your belief of my indifference?

JANE ONE: None at all. We all know him to be a proud, unpleasant sort of man; but this would be nothing if you really liked him.

JANE TWO AS LIZZY: I do, I do like him: I love him.

JANE ONE: [*a bit flat*] I could not have parted with you, my Lizzy, to anyone less worthy.

>   *Beat.*

> [*Spoken in a writing rhythm to the audience*] It is a truth universally acknowledged, that a single man in possession of a good fortune, must be in want of a wife.

ALL AS JANE [*sung a capella*]
>   And steal a look at Somebody, poor, dear Somebody,
>   Dear, sweet Somebody.

ACT THREE: 'DEAR JANE'

SCENE ONE: A SHORT SCENE

All JANES *are now* JANE.

ALL AS JANE: [*spoken; in echoes*] Dear Cassandra

JANE TWO: What dreadful hot weather we have!

JANE ONE: It keeps one in a continual state of inelegance.

JANE THREE: It began to occur to me before you mentioned it that I had been somewhat silent as to my mother's health for some time …

ALL AS JANE: [*sung with piano and harp with choreographed gestures*]
　　We bipeds, made up of frail clay,
　　Alas! are the children of sorrow; And, though brisk and merry today,
　　We all may be wretched tomorrow.

JANE TWO: [*spoken as music continues underneath*] but I thought you could have no difficulty in divining its exact state—you, who have guessed so much stranger things.

JANE ONE: She is tolerably well,

ALL AS JANE: [*sung with piano*]
　　For sunshine's succeeded by rain;
　　Then, fearful of life's stormy weather,

JANE THREE: [*spoken with music continuing underneath*] She would tell you herself that she has a very dreadful cold in her head at present …

ALL AS JANE: [*sung with piano*]
　　Lest pleasure should only bring pain,
　　Let us all be unhappy together.

JANE TWO: [*spoken with music continuing underneath*] But I have not much compassion for colds in the head.

ALL AS JANE: without fever or sore throat.

JANE ONE: I was sorry to hear that our cousin, Anna Lefroy is to have an instrument; it seems throwing money away.

JANE TWO: As to her playing it can never be anything.

ALL AS JANE: [*sung with piano and harp*]
 It appears from these premises plain,
 That wisdom is nothing but folly;
 That pleasure's a term that means pain,
 And that joy is your true melancholy.
 That all those who laugh ought to cry,
 That t'is fine frisk and fun to be grieving;
 And that, since we must all of us die,
 We should taste no enjoyment while living.

ALL AS JANE: [*spoken in echo music stops*] Cassandra …

JANE ONE: Mrs Hall, of Sherborne, was brought to bed yesterday of a dead child, some weeks before she expected, owing to a fright. I suppose she happened unawares to look at her husband. Affectionately yours, Jane

ALL AS JANE: [*sung with piano*]
 Let us all be unhappy together,
 Let us all be unhappy together,
 For sunshine's succeeded by rain;
 Then, fearful of life's stormy weather,
 Lest pleasure should only bring pain,
 Let us all be unhappy together!

> JANE THREE *begins pacing back of stage interspersing the line 'Dear Cassandra', and 'Martha' at random intervals and playing the violin. The other* JANES *begin to bring the scrunched-up notes back on the stage area reading them as they evoke the letters.*

JANE TWO: [*spoken*] Cassandra. Your letter took me quite by surprise this morning; you are very welcome, however, and I am very much obliged to you.

JANE ONE: I believe I drank too much wine last night at Hurstbourne;

JANE TWO: I know not how else to account for the shaking of my hand today.

JANE ONE: You will kindly make allowance therefore for any indistinctness of writing, by attributing it to this venial error.

JANE TWO: Your desiring to hear from me on Sunday will, perhaps, bring you a more particular account of the ball than you may care for, because one is prone to think much more of such things the morning after they happen,

JANE ONE: I was as civil to them as their bad breath would allow me, yours, Jane.

If I am a wild beast,

ALL AS JANE: I cannot help it!

JANE ONE: [*sung with sparse piano accompaniment and violin drone*]
Why fair Maid in ev'ry feature are such signs of fear express'd.

JANE TWO: [*sung as they wind the music box*]
Can a wand 'ring wretched creature,

JANE THREE: [*sung*]
with such terror fill thy breast.

JANE ONE: [*sung*]
Do my frenzied looks alarm thee

JANE TWO *and* THREE: [*sung; an echo*]
Do my frenzied looks alarm thee

JANE ONE: [*sung*]
trust me sweet thy fears are vain

JANE TWO *and* THREE: [*sung; an echo*]
trust me sweet thy fears are vain

ALL AS JANE: [*sung in unison*]
not for Kingdoms would I harm thee,
Shun not then poor Crazy Jane

JANE THREE: [*spoken*] Cassandra … Cassandra …

JANE ONE: [*sung*]
Still I sing my love lorn ditty,

JANE TWO *and* THREE: [*sung; an echo*]
Still I sing my love lorn ditty,

JANE ONE: [*sung*]
Still I slowly pace the plain,

JANE TWO *and* THREE: [*sung; an echo*]
Still I slowly pace the plain,

ALL AS JANE [*sung unison*]
Whilst each passer-by in pity
Cries God help thee, Crazy Jane

Last line sung in echoes as a choral round.

Beat.

JANE ONE: [*spoken*] I want to tell you that I have got my own darling Child from London. The Advertisement is in our paper today for the first time *Pride and Prejudice*.

JANE THREE: from the author of *Sense and Sensibility*.

JANE TWO: There are a few typical errors;

JANE THREE: and a 'said he,' or a 'said she,' would sometimes make the dialogue more immediately clear;

JANE ONE: but I do not write for such dull elves as have not a great deal of ingenuity themselves.

    Beat.

I must confess that I think Elizabeth as delightful a creature as ever appeared in print, and how I shall be able to tolerate those who do not like her at least, I do not know.

    Short pause.

JANE TWO: Martha has been all kindness.

JANE THREE: If I live to be an old woman, I must expect to wish I had died now,

JANE TWO: blessed in the tenderness of such a family,

JANE ONE: and before I had survived either them or their affection.

ALL AS JANE: [*sung with violin*]
    Are you lost to me forever, shall I see your face no more,
    Shadows fall, shadows fall, on the face that I adore, on the face
        that I adore.

JANE ONE: [*spoken straight to the audience*] Seldom, very seldom does complete truth belong to any human disclosure; seldom can it happen that something is not a little disguised,

ALL AS JANE: or a little mistaken.
    [*Sung*]
    Are you lost to me forever, shall I see your face no more,
    Shadows fall, shadows fall, on the face that I adore, on the face
        that I adore.

JANE ONE: [*spoken*] Pray remember me to everybody who does not inquire after me;

JANE TWO: those who do,

JANE ONE: remember me

JANE THREE: without bidding.

ALL AS JANE: [*sung*]

    Shadows fall, shadows fall, on the face that I adore, Shadows
        fall …

JANE ONE: [*sung*] Shadows fall on …

    Beat.

   [*Spoken*] If a book is well written,

    Brief pause.

   I always find it too short.

    Sudden cut to black.

THE END

Song 1. By Jane's Hand

Joan said to John

Luffman Atterbury

A

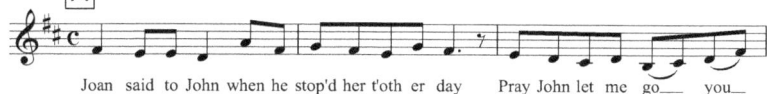

Joan said to John when he stop'd her t'oth er day Pray John let me go___ you___

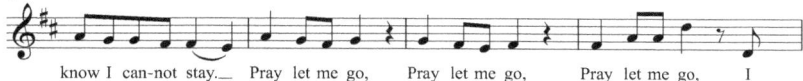

know I can-not stay.___ Pray let me go, Pray let me go, Pray let me go, I

B

can-not stay. You al-ways so tease me, and want me to stay, but tease me no more, for now I

must a - way. Tease me no more, Tease me no more, Tease me no more I

C

must a - way. So she left him in spite of all of all he could say, who

then___ could say nought but nay Joan, pri-thee stay, nay pri-thee

stay nay pri-thee stay pri-thee stay, nay Joan___ pri-thee stay.

Song 2. By Jane's Hand

It was a pleasant evening

for Piano

FAIRY DANCE HOLST
Arranged by EO

J3- It was a pleasant evening

J2-There were very few beauties, and such there were; were not very handsome

J3-Miss Iremonger did not look well, and Mrs Blount was the only one much admired

11

2

25 J1- she appeared exactly as she did in September, with the same broad face

J2- diamond bandeau pi- nk

J2- I traced in one the remains of the vulgar broad- featured girl
who danced at Enham eight years ago

J1,2,3- fat neck

J 2&3 The two Miss Coxes were there

hus band and

J3- the other is refined into a nice,
composed looking girl

J2-
Like Catherine Bigg

J1, J2. J3
She danced away with great activity

J1- Mrs Warren, I was constrained to think a very fine young
woman which I much regret

68

J1 - her husband is ugly enough, J2- uglier even than his cousin,

J 3- John,

j1, But he does not
look so very old

gliss

gliss.

Song 3 - By Jane's Hand

SHE NEVER TOLD HER LOVE

Joseph Haydn

Voice

F   C7   F   Bb   C7

She ne - ver told her love She ne - ver told her_

Voice

F   C7   F   C

love   But let con - ceal - ment   like a worm   in   the bud

Voice

F Bdim Cdim7 C G7   C   C   Bbm Edim

feed   on   her   da - mask   cheek   She   sat   like

Voice

Fm   Db7   C   Bb   F   Gm   F C

pa - tience   on a mo - nu - ment Smi - ling   smi - ling at_

Voice

Bdim7   C7   F   Gm   F C7 F

grief   Smi - ling   smi - ling at grief.

Song 4 - By Jane's Hand

THE IRISHMAN

William Shield
text by Robert Merry

(Penny whistle)

The Lon-don folks them-selves be-guile and think they please in a
(Jane 1)
(Jane 2)

ca-pi-tal style. Yet let them ask as they cross the street of a-ny young vir-gin they
(Jane 1)

hap-pen to meet. And I know she'll say from be-hind her fan, there's
(Jane 3)
(Jane 1)

none can love like an I - rish-man. There's none can love love love____
(ALL)

Like an I-rish-man like an I-rish-man there's none that can love like an
(+penny whistle)

I - rish - man

HOT CROSS BUNS

Children's rhyme
arr. attrib. Jane Austen

17

S. But if you have none of these lit-tle elves, these lit-tle elves,

A. But if you have none of these lit-tle elves,

B. But_ if you have none of these lit-tle elves, these lit-tle elves,

23

S. then you may eat them, then you may eat them, eat them, eat them,

A. then you may eat them, then you may eat them, eat them, eat them,

B. then you may eat them, then you may eat them, eat them, eat them,

29

S. eat them, eat them, then you may eat_ them all your selves.

A. eat them, eat them, then you may eat them all your selves.

B. eat them, eat them, then you may eat_ them all your selves.

Song 6. By Jane's Hand

FAINT AND WEARILY

Samuel James Arnold

Voice

Faint andwea-ri-ly the way-worn tra-vel-ler_plods un-chee-ri-ly a-fraid to stop;

Voice

(Mr. Nottley immediately dispatched a man and horse after the chaise)

wan - d'ringdrea-ri-ly, and sad un - rav'l-ler_ of the

Voice

ma-zes t'ward themoun-tain top; doubt-ing fear-ing while his course he's

Voice

steer - ing, cot-ta-ges ap- pear - ing as he's nigh to drop;_

Voice

(and in half an hour's time I had the pleasure of being as rich as ever; they were got about two or three miles off)

o how_ brisk-ly then the way-worn

Voice

tra-vel - ler___ threads the_ ma-zes t'ward the moun-tain top!___

SOMEBODY

anon.

VERSE 1

Voice

Were I ob-liged to beg my bread and had not where to lay_ my head I'd

5

Voice

creep where yo-nder flocks are fed_and steal a look at Some-bo-dy, Poor, dear,

10

Voice

VERSE 2

Some-bo-dy, Dear, sweet_ Some-bo-dy. Oh had I ea-gles wings to fly_ I'd

15

Voice

bend my course a - cross the sky and soon be-stow one lo-ving eye_ on

19

Voice

my a-dored Some-bo-dy, Poor, dear, some-bo-dy, Dear, sweet_ Some-bo-dy.

played with Ap Dulcimer in D

Song 8. By Jane's Hand

GOOSEY GOOSEY GANDER

Children's rhyme
arr. attrib. Jane Austen

Soprano: Goo-sey goo sey gan-der where shall I wan-der up-stairs down-stairs

Alto: Goo-sey goo sey gan-der where shall I wan-der up-stairs down-stairs

Bass: Goo-sey goo sey gan-der where shall I wan-der up-stairs down-stairs

S. in my La-dy's Cham-ber Old fa ther long legs would not say his prayers, Old fa ther

A. in my La-dy's Cham-ber Old fa ther long legs would not say his prayers, Old fa ther

B. in my La-dy's Cham-ber Old fa ther long legs would not say his prayers, Old fa ther long legs would not say his prayers, Take him by the left leg, take him by the

long legs would not say his prayers, Take him by the

long legs would not say his prayers,

left leg, take him by the left leg and throw him down - stairs.

left leg, take him by the left leg and throw him down - stairs.

Take him by the left leg and throw him down - stairs.

Song 9. By Jane's Hand

Begone Dull Care

trad. anon.

Be-gone dull care I pri-thee be gone from me Be-gone dull

Be-gone dull care I pri-thee be gone from me Be-gone dull

care you and I shall ne-ver a-gree Longtime hast thou been ve-xing me and

care you and I shall ne-ver a-gree Longtime hast thou been ve-xing me and

fain thou would'st me kill But in faith dull

fain thou would'st me kill But in faith dull

care thou ne - ver shall have thy will.

care thou ne - ver shall have thy will.

I HA'E LAID A HERRING IN SALT

trad. anon.

VERSE 1

Voice

(Jane 2)   (Jane 3)   (Jane 2)

I ha'e laid a her-ring in sa't, Lass gin ye lo'e me tell me now   I ha'e brew'd a

Voice

(Jane 1)   (Jane 3)

for-pit o' malt, an I can-na come il - ka day to woo. I ha'e a calf will

Voice

(Jane 2)   (Jane 1)

soon be a cow, lass gin ye lo'e__ me tell__ me now__ I ha'e a pig will

Voice

(ALL)   VERSE 2

soon be a sow, an' I can-na come il - ka day_ to woo. I've a hen with a

Voice

ha - ppi-ty leg Lass gin ye loe me tell me now Which il - ka day it

Voice

lays me an egg and I can-na come il - ka day to woo I hae a cab-bage up

Voice

on__ my shelf Lass gin ye loe__ me tell__ me now__ I downa eat it

Voice

all__ my-self and I can-na come il - ka day__ to woo.

Song 11. By Jane's Hand

WALY WALY

trad. anon.

(Violin Solo) ... O Wa-ly Wa-ly

up yon bank, and Wa - ly Wa - ly down yon__ brae, and

Wa - ly by yon ri - ver side where I and my love wont to__ gae. O

Wa - ly Wa - ly love is bon - ny a lit - tle while when

it is__new, but when its auld it wa-xes cauld, and wears a-way like

VERSE 2

mor-ning dew. When co-ckle shells turn sil-ver bells, and mus-sels grow on

ev - ry__ tree; when frost and snaw shall warm us a', then shall my love prove

true to__ me. But had I wist be - fore I kiss'd that love had been sae

ill to__wim; I'd lockt my heart in case of gold, and pin'd it with a

sil ver_ pin. Ah_____ Hmm_____

Song 12. By Jane's Hand

LET US ALL BE UNHAPPY TOGETHER

Charles Dibdin

Voice

We bi - pids made up of frail clay,
It appears from these pre-mi-ses plain,

A - las are the chil-dren of
That wis-dom is no-thing but

so - rrow; And tho' brisk and mer - ry to - day, We__
fo - lly; That plea-sure's a term that means pain, And that

all may be wre-tched to - mor - row; For sun-shine's suc - cee - ded by
joy is your true me-lan-cho - ly; That all those who laugh ought to

rain, Then fear - ful of life's stro-my wea - ther, Lest__
cry That tis fine frisk and fun to be grie - ving; And that,

plea-sure should on - ly bring pain; Let us all be un-hap - py to -
since we must all of us die, We should taste no en - joy-ment while

ge- ther, Let us all be un-hap-py to-ge-ther, Let us all be un-hap-py to-ge-ther, For
li- ving.

sun-shine's suc-cee-ded by rain; Then, fear-ful of life's stor-my wea - ther, Lest
(add lower harmony)

plea-sure should on-ly bring pain, Let us all be un-hap-py to - ge - ther.

Song 13. By Jane's Hand

CRAZY JANE

Harriet Abrams
text by Mr Lewis

19 — Voice: dit- ty still I slow-ly pace the plain whilst each pass-er by in

sing my love lorn dit - ty whilst_ each pass - er by in

23 — Voice: pi___ ty cries God help thee cra - zy Jane. cries God

pi___ ty (Jane 3) cries God help thee cra - zy Jane.

(Jane 2) cries God help thee cra -

26 — Voice: help thee cra - - zy Jane. cries God

cries God help thee cra - - zy Jane.

- - zy Jane. cries God help thee cra -

28 — (Repeat echos as needed) — Voice: help thee cra - zy Jane.

cries God help thee cra - - zy Jane.

- zy Jane. cries God help thee cra - - zy Jane.

Song 14. By Jane's Hand

ARE YOU LOST TO ME FOREVER

Che Faro - from Orfeo

Christoph Willibald Gluck

Melody

Are you lost to me for - e - ver shall I see your face no

Harmony

for - e - ver shall I see your face no

Voice

more Sha - dows fall___ sha - dows fall___ on_ the_ face that I___ a -

Voice

more Sha - dows fall___ Sha - dows fall___ on_ the_ face that I___ a -

Voice

-dore on_ the_ face that I___ a - dore (seldom...mistaken) Are you

Voice

-dore on_ the_ face that I___ a - dore

Voice

lost to me for - e - ver shall I see your face no more Sha - dows

Voice

for - e - ver shall I see your face no more Sha - dows

18

Voice: fall__ sha - dows fall__ on__ the__ face that I___ a - dore on__ the__

Voice: fall__ Sha - dows fall__ on__ the__ face that I___ a - dore on__ the__

22

Voice: face that I___ a - dore (pray...bidding) Sha - dows fall__ sha - dows

Voice: face that I___ a - dore fall__ Sha - dows

27

Voice: fall___ on__ the__ face__ that__ I___ a - dore__ on__ the__

Voice: fall___ on__ the__ face__ that__ I___ a - dore__ on__ the__

30

Voice: face that I___ a - dore Sha - dows fall__ sha - dows fall__ on__

SOLO

Voice: face that I___ a - dore Sha - dows fall__

LA MAMA

presents

BY JANE'S HAND

A whimsical window into the magnificent mind
of Jane Austen

Created by **Emma O'Brien**
with **Olivia O'Brien**

Crafted from the letters of Jane Austen,
Pride and Prejudice and songs of her time

La Mama Courthouse
17–28 July, 2024

FROM THE CO-CREATORS

"Seldom can it happen that something is not a little disguised, or a little mistaken."—Jane Austen

Jane Austen's life was censored by the patriarchy and romanticised by popular culture. Why did her family burn her letters? Of the 3,000 missives written by Jane, only 161 survive. How and why did she create? To explore these elements and 'reports' of Jane, we have delved into her letters, some of which are sharp tongued, others very much diary like, some deeply personal. We listened to and played songs from her personal music collection. Her music tastes were very broad, ranging from classical tunes to bawdy ale house songs. Finally, we immersed ourselves in her most famous novel, *Pride and Prejudice* and reimagined her creative process, by slowly breathing her characters in and wondering how did they evolve? We concluded that one actor was not enough to play the many sides of Jane Austen and have cast the show for three actors all playing Jane, and her characters from *Pride and Prejudice*, within a dreamscape.

PRODUCTION NOTES

The Text
All the text in this newly created/curated play is by Jane Austen, from her letters to her sister Cassandra, and from *Pride and Prejudice*. All the letters in this piece are selected for content and context and are not always presented chronologically. The dialogue from *Pride and Prejudice* has been chosen to give the audience a reimagining of her creative process by having those roles played by Jane herself.

The Music

We have woven in songs from Jane's private collection throughout the work. Music transcription was common in Jane's time. In her hand scribed collections, we found raucous folk songs, standard classical arias and dances. These pieces often had word substitutions by Austen and her own musical arrangements. All songs have been chosen to enhance, contradict, pre-empt, or refrain the spoken word in this exploration of Jane Austen's creativity.

The music for this original production is scored for piano, harp, violin, Appalachian dulcimer, shruti box, penny whistle and three voices. Songs are presented in lyrics only in the text with basic melodic transcriptions and chordal structures provided as a resource; listed here in order of play: 'Catch: Joan Said to John' (Luffman Atterbury), 'It was a Pleasant Evening' (after the *Fairy Dance* by Holst), 'She Never Told Her Love' (Josef Haydn), 'Irishman' (William Shield, text by Robert Merry), 'Hot Cross Buns' (trad children's), 'Faint and Wearily' (Samuel James Arnold), 'Goosey Goosey Gander' (trad children's), 'Begone Dull Care' (anon), 'I Ha'e Laid a Herring in Salt' (trad anon), 'O Waly Waly' (trad anon), 'Let Us All Be Unhappy Together' (Charles Dibdin), 'Crazy Jane' (Harriet Abrams, text by Mr Lewis), 'Che Faro' (Christoph Willibald Gluck).

Form and Style

Many writers and researchers have criticised portrayals of Jane Austen as being 'sweetened up', 'censored', 'romanticised'—including her theorised 'love life'. Even many of the adaptations of her novels have focussed on similar softer themes. This piece is actively avoiding both a romantic and anti-romantic framework. It does however acknowledge that Austen's commentary on her time in her novels, was not through rose-coloured glasses, but rather through a unique female perspective and an acerbic wit. This curated work is not meant to be a revelation about Jane Austen—or a new truth, but rather an immersion in elements of the enigma that is Jane and has been created/curated from an intergenerational feminist perspective. In this play we also honour the Austen tradition of home plays—acting out 'mini 'dramas' and 'tableaux' throughout.

We invite you, the audience, to step inside the magnificent mind of Jane Austen, bringing what you know about her, her novels, and her meaning, to the space; and maybe to discover more.

Acknowledgements

Thanks to the team at La Mama for all your extraordinary support in getting this new work up. Special thanks and to our friends and family for helping with this work. It takes a village to raise a child and a society to put on a piece of independent theatre! This work is dedicated to Maureen O'Brien (Emma's mother, Olivia and Henry's Nana). An avid and passionate reader, a writer, and worldwide traveller, Maureen shared her love of Austen with us all (yes, Emma is named after Jane's novel).

By Jane's Hand was first produced by Seldom Theatre at La Mama Courthouse Theatre, Melbourne, on 27 April 2023, with the following cast:

JANE ONE	Olivia O'Brien
JANE TWO	Isha Menon
JANE THREE	Marjorie Hannah

Lighting Design by Hannah Willoughby
Costumes by Susan Halls
Set Design by Dr Emma O'Brien OAM and Henry O'Brien
Sound Design by Dr Emma O'Brien OAM
Set Build by Martin Mason and Rod Connolly
Dramaturgy by Draf and Henry O'Brien

⊕ LA MAMA

CEO & Artistic Director – Caitlin Dullard
Marketing and Communications – Georgina Capper
Development & Pathways Manager – Myf Powell
Venue Technical Manager – Hayley Fox
Acting Venue Technical Manager – Shane Grant
Producer – Amber Hart
First Nations Producer/ Curator – Glenn Shea
Learning Producer & School Publications Coordinator –
Maureen Hartley
Ticketing & FOH Supervisors – AYA & Gemma Horbury
Design & Marketing Admin – Adam Cass
On-line Producer – Ruiqi Fu

Curators:
Gemma Horbury (**Musica**); Amanda Anastasi (**Poetica**);
Isabel Knight (**Cabaretica**); Sophia Constantine (**La Mama for
Kids**); Emma Fawcett (**La Mama Scratch**)
Documentation – Darren Gill

La Mama Theatre & Office is at 205 Faraday St,
Carlton VIC 3053
La Mama Courthouse Theatre, 349 Drummond Street,
Carlton VIC 3053

www.lamama.com.au   email: info@lamama.com.au
Facebook: lamama.theatre   twitter: LaMamaTheatre
instagram: lamamatheatre

Office phone (03) 9347 6948
Office hours Mon–Fri, 11am–4pm.

COMMITTEE OF MANAGEMENT: Richard Watts (Chair), Helen Hopkins (Dep Chair), Ben Grant, (Treasurer) Caitlin Dullard (Secretary), **Members** – Caroline Lee, David Geoffrey Hall, Kim Ho, Beng Oh and Mark Williams

La Mama Theatre is on traditional land of the people of the Kulin Nation. We give our respect to the Elders of these traditional lands, and to all First Nations people, past and present, and future. We acknowledge all events take place on stolen lands and that sovereignty was never ceded.

La Mama is financially assisted by Creative Victoria (Creative Enterprises Program), and the City of Melbourne (Arts and Creative Partnership Program).

We are grateful to all our philanthropic partners and donors, advocates, volunteers, audiences, artists and our entire community. Thank you!

CITY OF MELBOURNE

CREATIVE VICTORIA

DR EMMA O'BRIEN OAM
WRITER/DIRECTOR/ CREATOR

Emma (she/they) is the Co-Creator/Director of *By Jane's Hand* with her adult daughter Olivia. Emma has directed and edited award-winning music video clips, co-created and co-directed original works created with people living with cancer (*A Chorus of Women*, and *Opera Therapy* - subject of an SBS documentary). They are the founder and director of the Royal Melbourne Hospital Scrub Choir and the Global Scrub Choir. Emma recently returned from working on global video projects and performing in Geneva for the World Health Organization and at the UN in Geneva and New York, plus Central Park with Global Scrub Choir and at the Lincoln Centre premiering her new composition 'Deep Peace'. Emma is a theatre maker, director, writer, performer, singer, composer, music therapist, video editor, choir conductor and researcher. Emma loves swimming in the sea and has loved co-creating this work with their daughter Olivia even more.

OLIVIA O'BRIEN
JANE ONE

ISHA MENON
JANE TWO

Olivia (she/they) is a co–creator of *By Jane's Hand*, an actor, singer, instrumentalist, and stilt walker/street performer. They graduated from the University of Melbourne with honours in voice and has since pursued further education and a career in a diverse range of performance practices. Olivia has studied film and television with NIDA and has performed internationally at the United Nations in Geneva and New York City and in Central Park and Lincoln Center, singing alongside Sister Sledge and Ricky Kej. This is Olivia's first creative writing project with her mother Emma, and she has enjoyed the process of delving deeper into the words, music, and world of Jane Austen through a feminist lens.

Isha (they/them) is a curious and adventurous performer who makes theatre that is absurd and heartfelt. In 2019, they wrote, directed, and performed in a two-hander *girl walks home from a train* as part of the inaugural student-lead arts festival Discord held at the Victorian College of the Arts (VCA). After graduating from VCA in 2021, Isha had their Melbourne theatrical debut in 2022 in Red Stitch's work *Fast Food*, and that year they also wrote, directed, and performed in their first short film as part of Multicultural Arts Victoria's Ahead of the Curve commissions, Ammumma's House. They are super excited to be part of this gorgeous piece!

MARJORIE HANNAH
JANE THREE

Marjorie (she/her) is an actor, performer and soprano from Naarm who balances a diverse career of dynamic, ensemble-led creative work. Graduating in 2018 with a Bachelor of Music in classical voice from Newcastle Conservatorium, she is currently performing with The Song Company as an Emerging Artist and appears regularly with Divisi Chamber Singers, Alta Collective and the Consort of Melbourne. Her greatest joy is when devising and performing interdisciplinary works that meld the boundaries between dance, music, theatre, physical theatre, and performance art.

HANNAH WILLOUGHBY
LIGHTING DESIGN

Hannah (they/them) is a freelance technical operator. They have a degree in the Performing Arts and, as part of that course, trained under Bronwyn Pringle in lighting operations. They have since worked on multiple shows in theatre, comedy, clowning, variety, puppetry etc. They specialise in the weird and wonderful of the Melbourne theatre scene. They also work on the lighting team at MCEC, doing tech for less weird and wonderful corporate events.

STANDING OVATION FOR
AUSTRALIA'S HOME OF INDEPENDENT THEATRE

In 2024, La Mama celebrates 57 years of nurturing new Australian Theatre, fearlessly facilitating independent theatre making.

Built in 1883 for Anthony Reuben Ford, a Carlton printer, the original building in Faraday Street had been used as a workshop, a boot and shoe factory, an electrical engineering workshop and a silk underwear factory before becoming a theatre in 1967. It was established by Betty Burstall and modelled on experimental theatre activities in New York. Jack Hibberd's play *Three Old Friends* was the first play performed in the tiny space. Since that time the crowded intimacy of La Mama has provided welcome opportunities to a host of playwrights, actors, directors, technicians, film-makers, poets and comedians, such as David Williamson, Barry Dickins, John Romeril, Tes Lyssiotis, Lloyd Jones, the Cantrills, Judith Lucy, Richard Frankland, Julia Zemiro, and Cate Blanchett... the list of both new and experienced theatre makers, and those artists who have been nurtured there, is long.

I set La Mama up, as a space for writers and directors to perform in but also it was a space where people came, as audience, to participate in the creative experiment...

—Betty Burstall, 1987

La Mama Theatre—which on various occasions has been called headquarters, the shopfront and the birthplace of Australian Theatre—was classified by the National Trust in 1999.

The two-storey brick building is of State cultural significance because it has been occupied by La Mama Theatre... The building is indelibly associated with the performance arts and is a rare manifestation of an experimental theatre in Australia...
—National Trust Classification Report.

Sadly our home in Faraday Street burned down in May 2018 and, while we were in the process of rebuilding, our home was La Mama Courthouse on Drummond Street Carlton.

Happily, like a phoenix rising from the ashes, our rebuilt La Mama Theatre was reopened in December, 2021 with the War-Rak/Banksia Festival. (For rebuild details see https://lamama.com.au/rebuild-la-mama)

During its 50 plus years, La Mama has presented approximately 2,500 shows, and we now average around 50 primary production seasons annually, as well as developments, seasonal La Mamica events (Musica, Poetica, Cabaretica, Kids' shows), regular touring through our Mobile program, plus our VCE Learning productions, play readings, and many other special events.

Performances take place again in the restored La Mama, and continue at our second performance venue, the refurbished La Mama Courthouse, 349 Drummond Street.

An ever-increasing audience is drawn to La Mama productions, not only from the Carlton and Melbourne University environs, but from far and wide across the country.

La Mama continues to be an open, accessible space, actively breaking down barriers to the Arts through diverse programs, creative initiatives, affordable ticketing, improved accessible amenities and a welcoming ethos, for performers and audience alike, that has developed over the past five decades. La Mama is home to many and open to all.

For details of all productions and events, and bookings visit: www.lamama.com.au